Airplanes

Byron Barton

HarperCollins*Publishers*

For information address HarperCollins Children's Books, a division of HarperCollins Publishers,
10 East 53rd Street, New York, NY 10022.
Library of Congress Cataloging-in-Publication Data   Barton, Byron. Airplanes. Summary: Brief text
and illustrations present a variety of airplanes and what they do.   1. Airplanes—Juvenile literature.
[1. Airplanes]   I. Title.   TL547.B376   1986   387.7'334   [E]   85-47899   ISBN 0-694-00060-4
0-690-04532-8 (lib. bdg.)
12 13 SCP 15 14 13 12 11

In the sky

airplanes are flying.

This is a jet plane

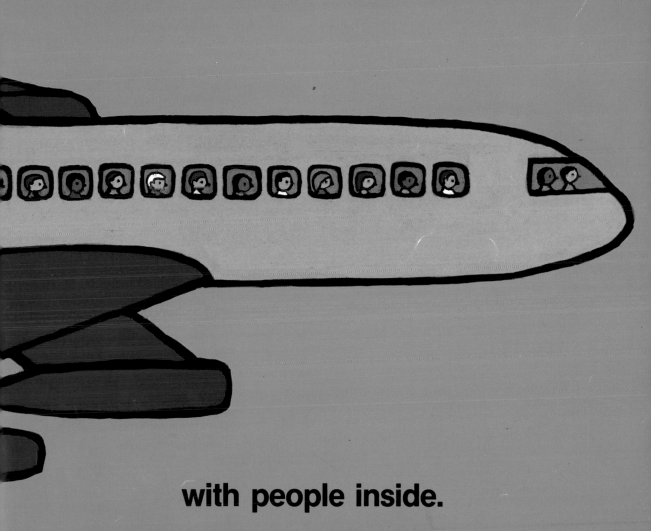

with people inside.

Here is a seaplane

landing on water.

There is an airplane

dusting the crops.

drink

There is an airplane

writing a message.

coming in for a landing.

Here are the passengers

loading trucks.

Here is the jet

leaving the plane.

These are workers

cleaning and checking.

Here is a truck

loading supplies.

Here are the people

getting on board.

There is the control tower.

Get ready for takeoff.

Here is the jet plane

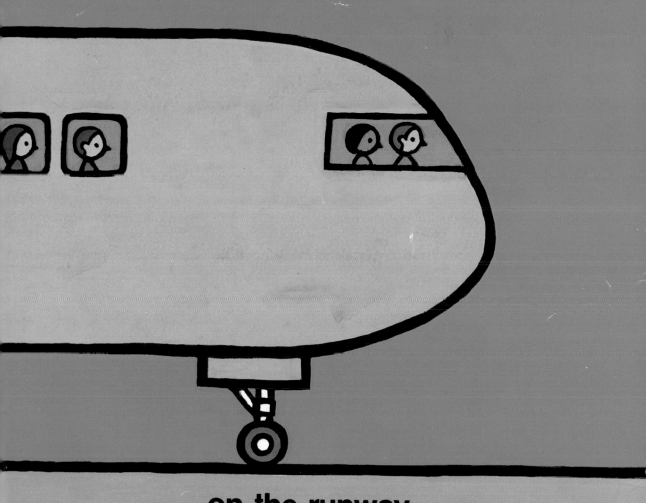

on the runway.

There goes the jet plane into the sky.